THE PUZZLE OF GOD

YOUR CROSS

ALAN COMEAUX &
RACHEL KLEIN

Your Cross

© 2020 Alan Ray Comeaux

All rights reserved.

No part of this publication in print or in electronic format may be reproduced, stored in a retrieval system, or transmitted in any form or by any means, electronic, mechanical, photocopying, recording, or otherwise without the prior written permission of the publisher.

All Scripture quotations, unless otherwise indicated, are taken from the Holy Bible New King James Version (NKJV)

Distributed by Bublish, Inc.

Paperback ISBN: 978-1-64704-075-8
eBook ISBN: 978-1-64704-096-3
Library of Congress Control Number: 2017916002

PRAISE FOR *YOUR CROSS*

"*Your Cross* is a wonderful understanding of God's will. Shockingly, I had no idea that Alan was ever homeless. Now, I completely understand his many years of financial pledge and physical support in helping us at The Samaritan Center."
–Betty S. Eskey, The Samaritan Center
Simi Valley, CA

"I enjoyed your book front to back! There are so many things that can go wrong and happen in a person's life…. This is like reading a better version of *Chicken Soup for the Teenage Soul*…. I hope to keep passing your book along in hopes that your word and struggle through life will help to open the eyes of others so they know they can do it. Just keep pushing through and trust in Gods to be there along the way. Thank you for sharing your life and book with the world."

–Twila, MD

"This book is worth the read. The writing is straight forward, no fluff, just the truth and real-life difficulties mixed with the beauty of God stepping into the picture and pouring out Grace. Alan's story inspires all believers to tell their story and should give non-believers hope in the midst of their struggle. Beauty from ashes, time and time again. Thank you, Alan."

–Wallace B.

"This book opened my eyes to a topic I've always avoided. My own cross. Love Alan's story and the lessons he endures. A MUST READ. Learn about yourself in the process. Thank you for sharing

–Ruben, PA

CONTENTS

Preface VII
Your Cross XI
Chapter 1 God's Laws 1
Chapter 2 Humble Beginnings 5
Chapter 3 A New Start 11
Chapter 4 Ye of Little Faith 17
Chapter 5 My God-given Talents 23
Chapter 6 The Love of My Life 29
Chapter 7 Broken Marriage 33
Chapter 8 God Spoke 41
Chapter 9 Money Was the Master 49
Chapter 10 Family Cross 53
Chapter 11 "Route 91" Country Festival. Why, God? 57
Chapter 12 The Puzzle of God 63
Acknowledgements 75
About the Author 79

PREFACE

Dear Reader,

Your Cross can be a true blessing in becoming closer to God. The cross killed our Lord and Savior Jesus Christ. He was crucified and buried for our sins. The use of the word "cross" is a metaphor for sin in my book. I petition you to write down your crosses in life with God. Study his Word daily and meditate on his glory and listen to his words and his direction. Welcome God into your life and you will have an abundant, blessed life with love, compassion, and the true understanding of "the puzzle of God." The "one word" God said to me changed my life forever.

Please read my story about my "crosses" and what God did for me.

–Alan Comeaux

Provide hope for the hopeless.
Provide dreams for the dreamless.
Provide directions to the lost.
Provide love where there is none.

YOUR CROSS

You will be born into a spiritual body.

You may like it or dislike it, but it will be yours for the entire period on Earth.

You will learn lessons.

You are enrolled in a full-time, informal school called life. Each day in this school, you will have the opportunity to learn lessons. You may not like the lessons or think them irrelevant or stupid.

There are no mistakes, only lessons.

Growth is a process of trial and error, experimentation. The failed experiments are as much a part of the process as the experiment that ultimately works.

A lesson is repeated until learned.

A lesson will be presented to you in various forms until you have learned it. When you have learned it, you can go on to the next lesson.

Learning lessons does not end.

There is no part of life that does not contain its lessons. If you are alive, there are lessons to be learned.

There is no "better than here."

When your "there" has become a "here," you will simply obtain another "there" that will, again, look better than here.

Others are merely mirrors of you.

You cannot love or hate something about another person unless it reflects something you love or hate in yourself.

What you make of your life is up to you.

Your answers lie within you. The answers to life are inside you. All you need to do is look, listen, and trust in God.

–Rachel Klein

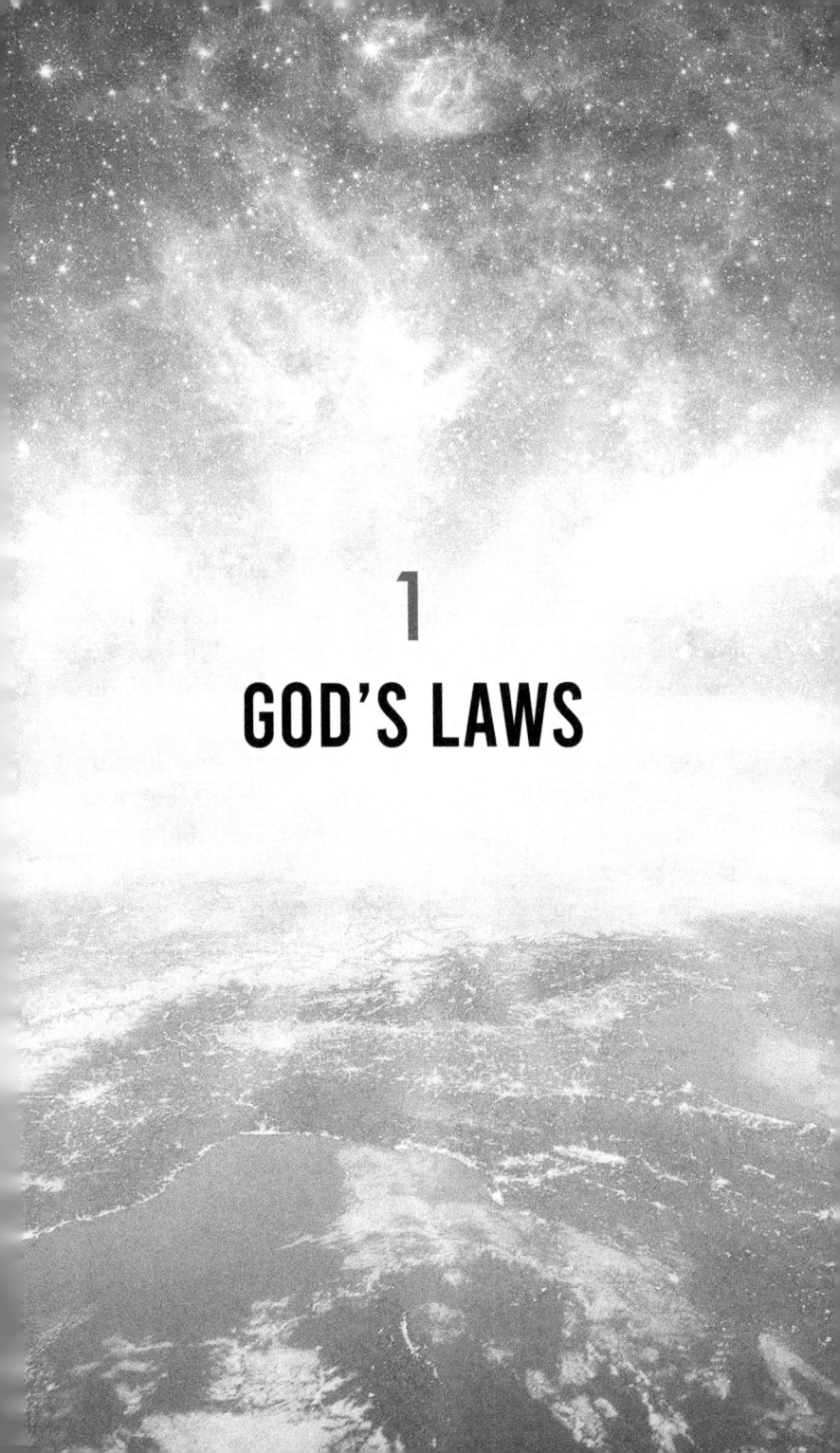

1
GOD'S LAWS

Your Cross
God law's for love, peace, and joy

God gave us laws to live by. When we have sin in our lives, we can never be free or happy. Our Founding Fathers wrote laws for our society. Most people don't even know that all the important laws were based on God's Ten Commandments. The Bible was written by God and transcribed by men. It holds the truth to life itself, and if we believe in these principles and follow these guidelines, we shall have happiness, abundance, and love for all.

The key is our internal belief systems and how those beliefs affect our lives–what we were taught and how we are wired. We are either wired with God or not. Can you make that distinction for yourself?

If the law is a reflection of God's character, and if humans are made in God's image, then the law fits human nature as well as that of God. It follows that humans are structured to follow certain laws and operate in certain ways. For instance, a truck that is not made for diesel fuel will not be able to run well on diesel. The truck might stop altogether with water or sugar in the gas tank. Likewise, if one runs full speed into a mountain, chances are that one will do more damage to himself or herself than to the mountain, because the mountain is stronger. If a person jumps from a plane, that person may feel as free as a feather for a moment, but unless he or she has a parachute, the law of gravity will bring him or her crashing to the ground.

God's law is like a manufacturer's manual, showing human beings how to act according to their nature. There are consequences to each action. People will experience brokenness or disintegration if they violate how God has made them. Breaking God's law is just like running into the mountain or jumping from the plane without a parachute. Unless individuals pursue an intimate relationship with God and with others, coming to know and employ their gifts, they will not experience wholeness. If we neglect or violate our nature, we will experience brokenness. God's law is meant to help His people avoid mistakes that lead to brokenness, not hurt them. It is intended to show the way to life and joy, not just to restrict.

What did Jesus mean when He said to take up the cross and follow Him?

> ***When He had called the people to Himself, with His disciples also, He said to them, "Whoever desires to come after me, let him deny himself, and take up his cross, and follow me." (Mark 8:34) (NKJV)***

Those who deny Him, are usually pursuing the Seven Deadly Sins:

- ***Pride*** *is excessive belief in one's own abilities. It interferes with the individual's recognition of the grace of God. It has been called the sin from which all others arise. Pride is also known as vanity.*

- **Envy** is the desire for others' traits, status, abilities, or situations.

- **Gluttony** is an inordinate desire to consume more than that which one requires.

- **Lust** is an inordinate craving for the pleasures of the body.

- **Wrath** is manifested in the individual who spurns love and opts instead for fury. It is also known as anger.

- **Greed** is the desire for material wealth or gain while ignoring the realm of the spiritual. It is also called avarice or covetousness.

- **Sloth** is the avoidance of physical or spiritual work.

Live without the Seven, and you will see Heaven.

2
HUMBLE BEGINNINGS

WALK OUT OF THE DARKNESS

My name is Alan Comeaux. I was born in Eunice, Louisiana, on December 1, 1965. We moved to Lafayette, Louisiana, when I was just a boy. My upbringing was normal for a kid in southern Louisiana. I was raised in a Catholic family with five kids: three girls and two boys. I was the first male born into the family.

I was raised by a military father, who later joined the oil business like so many southerners. We grew up in a middle-class family and went to Catholic schools and to church every Sunday.

What's amazing is that so many people who go to church do it out of tradition, not because of a will to do God's work. I find that we all want to say we are Christian, Catholic, or whatever your denomination is. We often contradict all rules of being true believers. I was a fake Christian, and in some ways, I still am–like most are. I was one who would go to church and do the opposite of what God calls us to do. After all, who was going to know, anyway? Yet God knows your story from beginning to end.

I was brought up in some very racially charged times. Being raised in the South, there was division and judgement for people that may not be the same race or color.

I went to Comeaux High School (yes, Comeaux is also my last name). There was a lot of fear early on in my teenage years. I remember going to the restroom with friends watching my back, in case we got jumped. There were many racial fights, and the police were called to the school many times. This was a way of life, being raised in the South; it was just very tense at times. I was always looking over my shoulder and was filled with anxiety.

My father was a great provider and worked hard for his family; I remember when things were bad he refused to take money from the government and went out and unloaded box cars to provide for his family. My father worked hard his entire life and always provided for all of our needs, however his one major shortcoming was alcohol. He would often solve his problems with rage and anger and still deals with anger to this day. All arguments involved elevated voices, followed by foul language and then reflection and forgiveness prevails as we all regret what we say and how we say it. Anger is a very hard thing to master, yet God says wherefore, my beloved brethren, let every man be swift to hear, slow to speak, slow to wrath. There was very little communication between my parents. They loved each other but never developed a way to truly speak to each other. I always felt like I was walking on eggshells, and I had a lot of anxiety at an early age. I felt like there was no control. Sometimes, I didn't want to be home at all, and I would disappear for days at a time.

My father, whom I love with all my heart, got help with his drinking. I know that, like so many of us, he regrets many of his actions. My father has great integrity and a heart of gold and loves people. I remember him pulling over so many times to help strangers who had problems with their cars. I loved that side of him. My father is a good man, and he has come to terms with his transgressions.

HUMBLE BEGINNINGS

My first job at the early age of fifteen, with my mother's help, I landed my first job at Tom's Drive-Through, where I mopped floors, washed the outside tables, and cleaned the place every day. After a few weeks, I got another job through a buddy for more money. I did not even give notice to the owner of Tom's that I had found a better job. I lived for myself, and I did not think I owed them anything, so I left. My mother later found this out. She was the key to my first lesson in humility and integrity. She made me go back to Tom's owner to apologize for my behavior and let them know I had gotten a better job. She understood the meaning of respect. My mother was patient–to a point–and gave me a foundation for God and respect for people. She used to say, "Don't make me break out with the broomstick." Yes, she would chase me with a broomstick, and she hit me on a few occasions when I got out of line. I used to grab the wooden handle from her and break it in half, and I would have to go buy her a new one right after. It sounds worse than it was. My mother was never afraid to discipline her children.

I was hired as a dishwasher, then a busboy, then a broiler's assistant, and–at the early age of seventeen–a cook. I was a very hard worker early on. It was instilled in me from my parents. I got things done, and there was no idle time at work for me. The weekday manager loved me, and he always wanted me to work his shift at night. When the night was done and the kitchen staff was cleaning up, I was the fastest closer in the kitchen. That meant we could all go home at a decent hour during the week.

I loved to work; that was my passion. I was very consumed by accomplishments, and I was always looking for bigger and better opportunities.

I moved out at almost eighteen, and I thought I had life by the short hairs. There will be so many crosses you will have to bear in life that will bring you closer to God. Unless you have never experienced God, it's hard to understand.

My mother, Rachel, has such amazing faith and wisdom; she would always have these "Rachelisms" that made me think about things bigger than myself. She always said *God will guide you*. I got my first real job making great money in the oilfield right after high school, a job that was hard to get unless you knew someone. My sister Cindy secured this job for me after she had worked there for a few years.

Welcome to Triumph Drilling Tools. I started off as an oil grunt. I did every single task I was asked to do. I had to grind paint off the floors for twelve hours a day for two months straight in a building the size of a football field. There were new colors for the company, and someone had to do it. Give it to the grunt. I did it with pride and never complained once.

I was then promoted to the pipe yard, which sounds like a prison term. After working in the yard and observing things, in a few short months, I saw a better way of doing things. I went home and mapped out a plan to improve our inventory and delivery system for the company.

Out of respect, I asked the existing yard manager at that time if I could show the boss a plan I developed for making the yard flow better. He agreed, as he was retiring very soon anyway. They call that "divine timing." My supervisor saw my plan and said for me to run with it. I came up with a new way of arranging the pipes and tools within the yard. I simply located the pipes and tools we sold the quickest to the front of the pipe yard. I created pickup zones and arranged the whole pipe yard based on what was rented the quickest.

HUMBLE BEGINNINGS

I streamlined pickup and delivery gates so that it was very efficient. Getting people to work with me and organizing things was easy–another gift of mine given to me by our Creator.

I was put in charge of the whole pipe yard when the other manager retired. I also got a pay raise. Then life happened.

Months later, the oil business took a turn, and layoffs started happening all over town and work dried up. *Well, there goes that,* I thought to myself. Not being in charge of your life sucks. You have no control over anything when you don't own your own destiny.

> **Jeremiah 29:11**
>
> 11 For I know the plans I have for you," declares the LORD, "plans to prosper you and not to harm you, plans to give you hope and a future.

I wanted a good life and was prepared to make a move. I packed up and left everybody I knew and moved to Studio City, California. I wanted to be in the movie business. I did not have a lot of money, which was a big mistake. It was culture shock, to say the least. It's expensive to live in California. I could not afford to live anywhere but my truck. First, last, and security? What the heck is that? Where I'm from, you give a man a deposit and move in over beers.

Welcome to homelessness.

I was running out of resources fast. I called my mom and asked her to make my truck payment, and she did so graciously. Times were tough and I know she did not have the money.

I parked behind a health club in Studio City. The owner of the health club was a retired studio hand. At $19.00 per month, it was a deal. He allowed me to use the health club as a command center. I did not have a cell phone back then, and the owner allowed me to give the number to the health club for interviews so that I could get messages. I explained my situation to him, and he let me monopolize three lockers for my belongings and gave access to hot showers anytime.

My first job was what God already prepared me for earlier in my life. I was working at a restaurant–La Express in Studio City. I asked the manager for increased hours so that I could save more money to get into an apartment of my own. I found a second job, too; however, it was kind of a far drive. I did not want to take this job, but something said to me, "Alan, take it," so I accepted. Welcome to Reseda Steak House.

Most people in California would not think that driving from Studio City to Reseda is very far. It's only 13 miles away. But I was set on working in Studio City, and my pride almost made me turn it down. The Holy Spirit told me to take it, so I made the commute every day to both jobs.

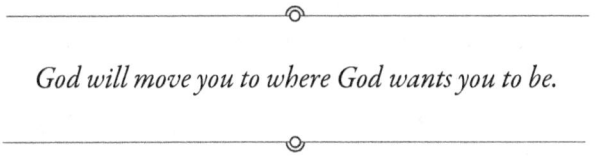

God will move you to where God wants you to be.

I did not have a bank account. I stored cash in my glove compartment. I had a plan, and life was great. I felt energized, motivated, and ready to take on the world. I would sleep in the bed of my truck, weather permitting. I had a roll-up foam mattress and a sleeping bag. I bought some foam earplugs to cut the noise out and bought a Walkman radio. That's right–a Walkman radio.

I was awakened one night by my truck moving and the sound of breaking glass. I jumped out of the back of my truck and surprised the thief, who was under the impression that the truck was empty. Have you ever seen an angry Cajun? Well, we don't ask questions, and I was not going to have a heart-to-heart with this

A NEW START

guy. I was raised with honor and the foundational belief that you never touch other people's belongings, much less destroy anything that is not yours. I was full of rage. I hit the guy right in the nose, and I'm pretty sure I broke it. He fell against the building as I grabbed him to hit him again. I suddenly felt a plunge into the middle of my back. It felt almost like being punched. I turned around to see another guy with a sharp object; I don't know if it was a knife or a screwdriver. As I turned around to defend myself and the first guy hit me with a construction claw in the head and I fell against my truck. They started to kick me as I got up and I ran between the building and my truck. The blood was rushing from my head and into my eyes.

They both were shouting that they were going to kill me. I rolled under my truck for protection in between the axles. They told me to stay there or they would kill me. Then I felt the blood against my shirt, and the pain set in immediately after that. I could feel the blood rushing out of my body, and I watched their feet from under my truck as they found my savings, my watch, my tapes, and anything of value.

They took everything but my *cross*, which was hanging from my rearview mirror. I never even thought about the *cross* hanging from my mirror. I had just installed that crucifix to satisfy my mother. The cross never left me. I find that interesting that all worldly things were taken, but I was left with my *cross*.

The thieves left me bleeding under my truck. I waited for a minute or two to make sure they were gone, and then I dragged my body from under my truck. My back was soaked in blood at this point; I took some T-shirts and balled them up, applying pressure to my back and head as I drove myself to the hospital.

YOUR CROSS

I went to the emergency room, where I was stitched up, filed a police report, and was finally discharged. Why God? Why would you allow this to happen to me? Free will is granted to all and not the will of God.

4
YE OF LITTLE FAITH

Do you need to be sold? Are you still looking to buy in to the idea of God? Are you debating if it's a good idea to believe?

God is faith! But without faith, it is impossible to please Him: for He that cometh to God must believe that he is, and that he is a rewarder of them that diligently seek him. (Heb. 11:6) (KJV)

This is an incredible statement–yet, it is in the Bible! Take it for exactly what it says. Just think–anything a person does, in attempting to be Christian, means absolutely nothing if he lacks faith. For without faith, he has no hope–no possibility of pleasing God. That is serious! Consider yourself: Do you have real faith? Is it sufficient for salvation?

My cross was so heavy, I could not bear it. It sucked the life right out of me. I was angry and defeated and full of pride. God was not in my life. I felt desperate and alone. I was ashamed of my life. I was scared, and no local support or family I could count on to help me. I needed help but was too proud to ask for it. Pride was a "cross" I needed to fix. Pride almost killed me and was a terrible thing in my life for a long time.

After being robbed and stabbed, sleeping in my truck took its toll on my body over the next few days. I felt emotionally drained and got very sick. I had no money and only enough gas to get to my job in Reseda.

I called my mom and told her I had a little fever and that I was not feeling well. A mother's intuition never fails, and she begged me to come home. I said nothing about being stabbed, because I did not want to worry her. I said, "I am going to stick it out, but I love you." She still remembers that call very vividly. She knew that something was wrong and had been praying for me since I had left Louisiana.

I parked my truck behind one of the restaurants. I was met by Ralph Hine, the owner. He stopped me at the entry and said, "Alan, what happen to you? You don't look very good. Are you OK?" I lost it and broke down. I didn't have the words or energy to explain it. I was embarrassed to be living in my truck. I felt like a kid who had done something wrong and wanted to keep it all inside. I was in pain from head to toe and really embarrassed about what I had become.

God took the foolish pride right out of me. Charlene, Ralph's wife, walked in as I was bawling and confessing my cross. Charlene is a very leery person in general. She was a very stern businesswoman and not easily impressed.

They both agreed to help me get the medical attention I needed. After this, I was not expecting Charlene to welcome me into their home, let alone, offer me a place to live. I was allowed to sleep in a normal bed for the first time in many months. Clean clothes, a refrigerator, warm bedding, TV, and a soft pillow–so many things we take for granted.

YE OF LITTLE FAITH

I will never forget what Charlene said to me before she closed my door. She said, "I saw your *cross* hanging from your rearview mirror. You know, Alan, God works though people." Have faith in him and all will be given.

The only thing left in my empty truck. That's amazing grace.

That struck me as odd, and the hair on my arms stood up. My mother believed in God. She introduced me to God, yet I did not believe in a God. Where are you God? I said that so many times after this. I was angry with God. Now God was on my to-do list daily. I said the Lord's Prayer daily. Our father which art in heaven and "three Hail Marys". I grabbed that cross in my truck as I said each prayer and committed to God daily. Church was a priority for me every Sunday. It worked to move me in God's direction to greater things. I have said it every day on my way to work for the last 32 plus years and give thanks for all the good in my life.

God works through people, places, and things. Ralph and Charlene could have just been good Samaritans, but I believe that the job I originally hadn't wanted had saved my life. God places you where you should be, which I know because of my mother's influence and Charlene's comment that someone was watching over me. God was watching over me with the spirit of faith from others who believed. My mother was a prayer warrior.

All these crosses make you who you are. God makes it all new again, with faith and the understanding that all bad things work for the greater good to bring you closer to God and God's work.

Ralph Hine was later diagnosed with colon cancer. God put me in his life for a reason, too. A piece of my puzzle was found with the Hine family. I was always a great caregiver. That's something I did not realize for a long time. I love to serve people. I guess I feel very necessary and whole when I serve others. I was there to help Charlene with Ralph, taking him from the bed to bathroom and outside for fresh air. His weight was only seventy-five pounds before his death.

I was there during some very dark days with Charlene; she had no children of her own. I will always love the Hine family for what they did for me. I am forever grateful.

5
MY GOD-GIVEN TALENTS

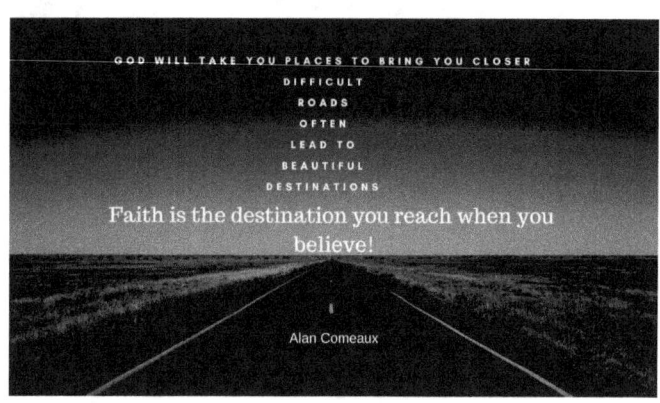

I have an acronym for the word Life.

Living In Fear Everyday–Without God, there is fear, and with God, there is courage and living with a daily purpose to love God and love people.

Anybody who knows me personally knows that I can sell anything, another gift given to me by our Creator. I got a telemarketing job selling matrix ribbons in 1987. That led to becoming one of the top sales experts in the office-supply industry. After thirty-two years, I'm still the top salesperson in the company I helped build United Imaging Inc. I now have my own sales division in Simi Valley, California. I have trained more than fifty salespeople under me. I have sold over $180 million in products and real estate combined all over the United States. I have over $200 million in combined sales experience–all by telemarketing, one of the hardest jobs there is. We've landed accounts like the White House, Disney, AT&T,

eBay, and many more. I did this by immersing myself in learning and ongoing education.

God wants you to achieve and grow.

I would always look for better ways to do my job. This gift of salesmanship has given me an incredible life that continues to bless me in many ways. It has also helped me grow financially and helped others change their lives.

I also got into real estate with the income that I earned. Real estate was my mother's idea for investments. She was a realtor in Lafayette, Louisiana. My mother was my mentor on savings, investments, and spiritual guidance. She taught me the rule of seventy-two (a simple way to determine how long an investment will take to double given a fixed annual rate of interest) She also told me how to save capital and tithe 10% of income to a greater cause. This can enrich your life 10 fold by giving back I am living proof of that. I started to buy and sell houses, and that became a separate business for me. I flipped homes in Florida, Louisiana, and California for many years to come. I had a unique ability to see potential and buy things correctly in a market upswing. I kept some homes when I got a great deal. I became a landlord at a very early age. I realized that real estate was a great asset if you buy it right. Properties produced a good income stream and tax benefits. I built companies, established LLC for properties learn a lot about business.

MY GOD-GIVEN TALENTS

When you are doing well, you tend to forget about God. Up to this point, I was very faithful with church attendance but started to replace God with worldly things. Don't lose touch with God. He will bring you back to the cross. I drove beautiful cars and bought houses–yes, multiple houses–at a very early age. I was more successful than most people around me. My life was about accomplishments, and I worked very hard in a lot of ways not to return to that truck on the streets. That blind ambition leaves you empty and lonely without God.

You cannot make money your master. You must choose God over wealth. I have learned that the love of money is a sin in itself. There is nothing wrong with money by itself. God wants you to have an abundant life. However, money can be used for good or bad things in your life, and it can be addictive and foster sin.

Christ-I-A-N

(I Am Nothing) without Christ!

–Rachel Klein

Our greatest

wealth is

our health!

We squander

health

in search

for wealth.

We scheme,

toil, and save,

then squander

wealth

in search

for

health

But all we get is a grave!

–Rachel Klein

6
THE LOVE OF MY LIFE

In 1995, I found another piece of my puzzle. I met my beautiful wife, Sandra Campiani. We dated for three years, and she then became pregnant with my son, Brandon. Sandra had a beautiful daughter named Vanessa, who I fell in love with. She was my little girl.

Vanessa was the most gorgeous little girl on this planet and was such a blessing to me back then; to this day, she has such wisdom and is super intelligent. She gives me great advice and I have learned to be a better father to my children. Both of them have helped me realize that I am imperfect and my tone and what I say to them affects the results of my message. I have learned that they are very different people than I am. They need to be understood individually. They have different personalities and feelings. All things should come from love for them. We all want to be loved and understood. This took me a long time to learn. My family cross was a lesson that took many years for me to learn. God will never give up on you. He will bring that cross back to you until you have learned the lesson.

Brandon was born on February 22, 1999. I had a perfect little family, a boy and a girl. That was my dream, and this was a very happy time in my life. Brandon was a happy baby and laughed all the time. I was not an experienced father and did not have all the answers as we all struggle to have that balance only God will bring you though time. My children have taught me patience, love and acceptance.

My family lived in, as my wife called it, "the bachelor pad" in Box Canyon in the Chatsworth Hills. The Manson family used to hide and live up in those hills. I did not know that until I bought the place, of course. It was full of crazy people from the sixties.

I fell in love with the place. It had a beautiful rocky sandstone stream in the back of the house that would flow during the winter, leading to a beautiful waterfall that you could see from one of our sixty windows.

The place was like a zoo, really. It had all types of wildlife: horses, sheep, bobcats, raccoons, squirrels, mountain lions, and many other of God's animals. It was a three-story redwood home and had beautiful tongue and groove for walls and ceilings–a perfect pad for someone single. Unfortunately, this home was not suitable for children.

Sandra and I got the itch and moved into a larger place in Simi Valley. I kept the canyon property and rented it out for years and then eventually sold it.

We got married July 1, 2000, making it official in God's eyes. It was a wedding I will never forget, with lots of family and friends. It took place in Woodland Hills at Saint Bernardine of Siena Catholic Church, and the reception was in Malibu, on the beach. I was very much in love with my wife and my new family. Life was great.

Can't take vacation

From a vocation!

All part of our cross!

God won't channel

What I can't handle!

Cross not heavy to bear unless I

forget God's there!

A fruit from the Holy Spirit–joy!

J (Jesus)

O (Others)

Y (You)

Reverse the curse,

put God first!

Cross takes us

everywhere–north, south,

east, and west!

I travel easy

by

way of prayer!

My vehicle

is faith.

–Rachel Klein

A perfect marriage is about two imperfect people that refuse to give up on each other.

Years later, like all marriages, my marriage with Sandra struggled. I lost my way again with God and pride.

We had some real differences, in my opinion, on parenting, money management, and meeting each other's needs and never talked about our past. She decided to leave our home and separate for a while. I was working so much back then; we would just pass each other and not have real conversations. I was shocked she wanted to move out. I have to admit, back then I was young and cocky, and I was never easy to talk to. To me, she left the marriage when she wanted to move out. I did not know at that time that Sandra wanted a break and separation; she did not want a divorce. We really did not know each other's concerns about relationships. Sandra and I never dove deep about all the things that haunted us as human beings. Our past experiences can and will kill a marriage and any relationship. You have to talk about it on a much deeper and open level. As humans we bury our emotions and the past. We just want to forget about the bad things that effect our emotions. We are all broken and insecure. We just want to be loved and accepted.

She started to stay out late. When she went out with friends, she didn't go out like a married woman. She acted like a single person, in my eyes, which led to a lot of our arguments. I wish I had had the wisdom and patience to talk to her about her past pain that was never voiced. I was hurt and mad, and my pride, anger, and spitefulness took over. I said that if that's what she wanted, I would give it to her. I immediately found a house for her. I packed her stuff and moved her out of our home. When I was in pain, I just took action. I finished what needed to be done and moved on.

Unpack in your relationships.

We all have this emotional baggage we never unpack. Sandra had emotional baggage from her previous marriage. I came to find out later in more detail that her ex was a liar and a cheater, the worst kind of man there is. He was also involved with some very shady people. Sandra had lived a very sheltered life with her parents, and her ex had been her only way to move out of her parents' home.

Unpack in your relationships. If you can't talk to your spouse, write him or her a letter about what your fears are. Your spouse needs to know what you feel and felt about your past relationships. Unpack the negative emotions, and express what happened and how that made you feel. Do it! He or she needs to know.

I believe that Sandra, because of those experiences with her ex, thought all men would cheat on her. She did not want to relive it. So, staying out late and pushing me away was about her past experiences with men. She would sabotage her relationship with me because of her unresolved fear. In Sandra's subconscious, I was never going to love her, and that history would repeat itself.

We fear whatever has already happened to us. That was a "fear fact" that was never unpacked. We need to voice all fears going forward in any new relationship. If we begin new relationships without unpacking our baggage, they will be over before they start.

We need to unpack those negative feelings and *trust* in new relationships. We all do this unconsciously to protect ourselves from pain. I wish I had known more about her pain with men. I wish I had been able to talk to her in a way to understand her pain. Not me–I had way too much pride.

I served Sandra with divorce papers months later. I had met someone new, and it was time to move forward. This new person seemed to be the polar opposite of Sandra, and I only thought of my needs. Me, me, me–that was pride talking. I thank God that things moved very slowly with this new person.

Sandra was taken aback by this decision, and her reality was shattered by this. She couldn't believe she could be replaced so quickly. We all can be replaced; don't ever think it's one-sided. I did not try to understand her pain until much later. I never stopped to think about what she had gone through in her past. When I saw her, I gave her no sympathy or patience. She cried on so many occasions. Sandra did not want a divorce, and she vocalized that. However, I was done with this relationship.

My pride told me, "You are not right for me. You left the marriage, so you can move on with your life, because I have." One night, I got a call from Sandra's uncle, who was a pastor. He told me that Sandra was on an altar in church, begging God for forgiveness. She cried for three hours on that altar. I did not care one bit. She had made her bed, and she could lie in it.

My baggage was not unpacked either. I had also been cheated on, and I pushed her away to protect myself. To be honest, I thought she had met someone else. She tried everything to get me back in her life, but I was not having it. I had grown up in a hostile environment with lots of arguments, and for me, running was the best solution at the time. I never told her about being stabbed, and not once did I have any discussions about my past and my fears. All this was blocked for me, and I never worked through my childhood issues. I never unpacked any of it. We did not truly know the other's stories.

My neighbors, Roy and Kim, were a Christian family and helped me go back to church. Roy was at my house every day, praying for me and talking to me about marriage. I really did not care about anyone's opinion. Pride was my sin. There were so many faithful people in my life. There were plenty of people praying for us. Weeks went by, and Sandra and I would talk from time to time. I felt like I had the power.

We create our own drama without God in our lives.

Then there was one phone call to Sandra that was very different.

Sandra surrendered her life to God on this matter. On that altar, I am telling you, she was touched by God. At her weakest moment, she confessed to God and begged for forgiveness. Sandra had left it up to God. I talked to her, and this time she was not a sad little girl anymore. She had God's strength and faith in her voice. There was no fear or nervousness–after all, she had the most powerful person on her side. She said with certainty, and I felt it to my core, "Alan, I love you, but this is not in my control anymore. It's all up to you, and I wish you well. I will always love you."

It was powerful–that is all I can say. I still remember how chilling it was to me. Her voice conveyed love, not anger, regret, or pride. Sandra was at complete peace. I hung up, a little confused by how strong she had been. She had mentioned God so many times, and there I was again, reflecting on God. *What does God have to do with this?* I thought. I found myself lost again, not focusing on his laws and beliefs.

My mother flew into town while all this was happening, and she knew me better than anyone. My mother is a very spiritual lady and is truly blessed by our Creator. She asked me what had happened with Sandra.

She asked, "What needs did she not meet? What caused the marriage to end?" She asked about the new woman as well. Through this whole thing, she was never judgmental. Mom asked me to take a swim, so we got in the water and talked about all the issues I had been having with Sandra. We create our own drama without God in our lives. My reasons were prideful and not valid reasons to divorce my wife. In the godliest way, my mom said, "Alan, I have listened to you completely, and I love you as Sandra does. Sandra is your wife, and you have chosen her. You have chosen her to be your wife, and she is remorseful for her decision. She meets your needs, and you have to take responsibility for your part in this marriage. This new woman in your life is the forbidden fruit. The devil wants division in your family."

That really sunk in. It was like the devil himself put her in my life, and in my eyes, it was meant to be. In God's eyes, this person was a test. Mom's words hit me hard, as if God were talking though her. She was a very faithful lady and, to this day, has tremendous wisdom. I was fixed on my mom's words. It was very spiritual when she spoke.

"Sandra loves you, son, but maybe she can't talk to you. You are not an easy man to deal with sometimes. You have a heart of gold; however, you take great pride in being right all the time. I am here to tell you that Sandra loves you. What you need to understand and come to terms with is that pride has something to do with this decision.

"You have a beautiful life that God has blessed you with. You have two beautiful children who depend on you, and you need to let pride go. You need to understand your vows are 'til death do you part. Do what God wants and not what you want."

Seeing the world and God as a puzzle?

When mass first starts, the lector is holding the Word of God, followed by the altar boy carrying the cross.

I call that a

crossword puzzle.

–Rachel Klein

8
GOD SPOKE

LOVE WINS

In the water, up to my waistline, I heard God say, "Repent." I felt touched and moved by something I can't even explain. The word was in my heart before my head. I didn't even know what "repent" meant, but my actions and body did exactly that. It was a voice that was familiar to me. A soft whisper I felt in my heart and soul. I felt instant remorse. Just to be clear about what repent means, it is to feel or express sincere regret or remorse about one's wrongdoing or sin. You need to listen to God when God talks.

The first demand of Jesus' public ministry was, "Repent." He spoke this command indiscriminately to all who would listen. It was a call for radical inward change toward God and man.

I immediately felt shame and regret, and God took that pride right out of me again—just like when I was broken, stabbed, and left to die on the streets. I remember that completely humble feeling that takes over your soul and blesses you at the same time. I cried as all this pride left my mind and body. It was very powerful. We all want to be loved and accepted for who we are, and that was another lesson about pride. It's the killer of all relationships. Another piece of my puzzle.

God resists the proud but gives grace to the humble.

We are warned many times in Scripture to stay clear of pride and remain humble before the Lord, but far too often, the person with a prideful attitude is the last one to know it.

This creates a problem because unlike many other sins that we commit, pride is very sly in the way that it creeps into our lives undetected. We often have no warning signs other than the voice of the Holy Spirit, which we often dismiss as wayward thoughts. There can be many causes for pride.

Some people will get a spirit of pride because they are putting up defense mechanisms to try to make up for a deficiency they feel they have when comparing themselves to others.

The Bible says in Proverbs 16:18, "Pride goeth before destruction and a haughty spirit before a fall." As Christians, we have to keep watch over our attitudes towards ourselves and others.

We might find it easy to find faults in others, while blindly allowing a spirit of pride to live within us (1 Peter 5:5–6, KJV).

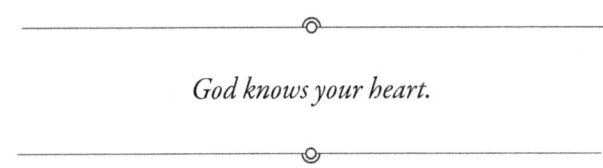

God knows your heart.

He can only work through you when your heart is pure. The heart is where God lives. You can't change your heart unless you change your ways. You can think and say, "I am not going to use drugs, drink, watch porn, commit adultery, overindulge, lie, steal, or covet," but your heart says, "Yes, I am."

You can hide from all but not from God. When you associate pleasure with the things that are evil in your life, you have made the choice to continue with that path. This is where your heart is. God will not hear you unless you are faithful. If you associate the things in your life that are not good with pain, then you have made a good choice, and your heart will follow.

The pain affects your parents, friends, loved ones, yourself, and God. The pain affects your body, mind, and spirit. True change starts with your heart. Be diligent with every moment, and consult God with your heart's decision. You will be heard.

I immediately called this other woman to tell her I couldn't see her anymore. I needed to get my marriage straight. I apologized and hung up. I called my wife and said, "Listen, I am sorry, and I want to talk to you today. I am not seeing this other woman, and I'm so sorry I hurt you."

Sandra was not the same woman, she said, point blank. "Why have you changed your mind now?" she said calmly, with power. I proceeded to tell her what I had experienced. I was the one begging now. She had God on her side. It was very humbling for me. I drove over there immediately and proceeded to have the first real conversation about our marriage and our experiences.

We talked for hours and decided together to really become close and work on our relationship and our relationship with God. Sandra was so passive and humble. I felt the love and patients she expressed with me. She and I were truly touched by God, and we were humbled by this whole experience.

I was always in love with Sandra, but I fell in love with her very deeply that day. It was a blessing in so many ways. She was always the one for me. God blessed our unity but needed to teach us both about respect and honoring our vows. Anyone who knows my wife can verify she is an angel. I am very blessed and lucky to have her as my wife.

We moved back in together, and life became blessed again. We joined a new church and started to go on a regular basis, with God in our lives. Realize that only God–and not your spouse–can meet your emotional needs. The key I have found its putting their needs before you own.

Encourage your spouse with the words,
"I love and accept you for who you are,
not who I've been trying to make you become."

The Bible calls you to still respect and appreciate your very imperfect spouse. This is true whether you're a husband or a wife.

On March 26, 2014 my wife–my "life"–was diagnosed with multiple sclerosis, an incurable disease. I found out through my experience with the Hine family that I am a great caregiver. God has prepared me for this already. His wisdom is so inspiring.

Pride
Petty
Regretful
Ignorant
Desperate
Evil

–Rachel Klein

No MasterCard. Try a MasterLord.

Our Soul
Is Our Silver
and Gold! Saint
Peter in the Book of Acts
says to the man at the
Gate. Silver and Gold
I have not but in the name
of Jesus, pick up your
palette and walk! That
Was Faith
At TEMPLE'S
GATE!
Christians
Listen to the
Prophet
Not PROFIT!

–Rachel Klein

9
MONEY WAS THE MASTER

The almighty God or the almighty dollar which do you worship?

I had a super opportunity in 2008. I took almost a million dollars that I made from real-estate flips and invested it into a fund called the GLR Fund, which my accountant of twenty years, I trusted him with my money. I saw the returns–they were over 17 percent. I talked to many investors, doctors, lawyers, and some very smart businesspeople.

I trusted my accountant which I will not mention his name, who had worked for some very large accounting firms. I pulled the trigger and invested a large chunk of my assets. I continued to get quarterly statements for years, and all was looking great. It's also known as GLR Capital Management.

One day, a letter came from the U.S. Department of Justice, notifying me that GLR was being investigated by the SEC. As it turns out, the fund was a Ponzi scheme. My heart stopped beating–my wife and I could not believe it.

God just does not want you to make money your master.

I was driven by money again and had not been connected to God in my decisions. I did not pray on this matter. Greed, pride, and cockiness took over. I was focused on one thing: money. Overall, they took over sixty million dollars from investors.

Let me make something super clear about God: money is not evil. God wants you to have money and all the fruit to be plentiful in this world. God just does not want you to make money your master. Some of the richest people in the world do great work with their money to serve the better good, and that's in the message. You must focus on the greater good of people around you and use your resources to serve others. I have met so many people with money who are miserable. There is no happiness, no joy, and no satisfaction in their lives. Money truly does not make you happy. You need to be spiritual, grounded, and connected with your Creator.

These three individuals—one being my accountant—are all serving time now. Each got up to fifteen years of prison time. God will prevail. God has already served justice, in my eyes. In retrospect, it was the best thing that ever happened to me.

Years of my hard work were focused on money, yet God had a plan. God gave me money and took it away, just like that. You can't worship God and money; you must choose. I choose God first in all my decisions.

According to Proverbs, a fool and his money will duly part.

What is a fool? A fool is someone who is dense and arrogant. He cannot be instructed in any way. His motto is "Don't confuse me with the facts; I have my own opinions." In fact, the fool delights in airing his opinions. If challenged on his opinions, he is often quick to lose his temper. His hard-headed, foolish ways shame his parents. In Proverbs 14–15 and in other chapters, wise King Solomon warns his audience about such people. To be honest, most of us have acted foolishly at one time or another. I will put God first in all my decision for the rest my life.

I will accept any cross that comes my way with joy and happiness. I have had smaller crosses in my life that reflect my obedience and humbleness to all and God. The most important thing is having faith. It's all a lesson for the greater good of your relationship with God. Proverbs 21:5 the plans of the diligent lead surely to abundance, but everyone who is hasty comes only to poverty.

10
FAMILY CROSS

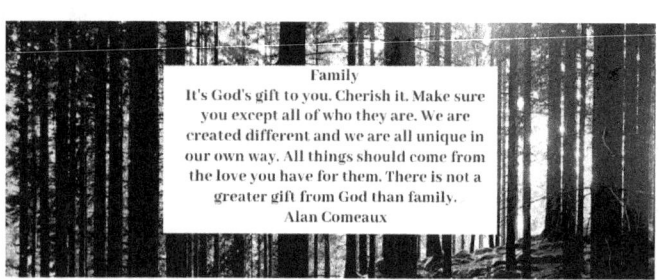

Family
It's God's gift to you. Cherish it. Make sure you except all of who they are. We are created different and we are all unique in our own way. All things should come from the love you have for them. There is not a greater gift from God than family.
Alan Comeaux

Your "Tone": Teaching Others Negative Energy

Our tone of voice can be taken negatively. How you talk and how you express yourself are more important than the message.

Anger should wait and has no place in your delivery. If you are an angry person, you need to ask, which parent did I learn that from? If you learned it, you will pass it on to your children, so remove it from your life.

> ***Know this, my beloved brothers: let every person be quick to hear, slow to speak, slow to anger; for the anger of man does not produce the righteousness of God. (James 1:19–20)(KJV)***

> ***Fathers, do not provoke your children to anger, but bring them up in the discipline and instruction of the Lord. (Ephesians 6:4)(KJV)***

I still carried the cross of parenting. I was a very strict father, making sure my kids worked for everything. That is a not a bad thing by itself. I let them know the value of hard work and discipline. You could say I ruled with an iron fist. I learned you need to talk to your children in a loving way. I was never taught how. I was taught to yell. I thought this is how I was raised, so it must be correct. Wrong!

My children feared me, much like I had feared my father. I really believed that was how you raise your kids. You know, for years I really had no idea how to raise kids, or for that matter talk to them. How to communicate effectively is key. It's not what you say; it's how you say it. I regret deeply that I did not have patience with my children at times. I let my anger get the best of me, they are just loving children. You mold them the way you raise them.

Do not provoke them to anger, ever. If you talk to your children with anger, you will raise angry adults. If you teach your children to be abusive, you will raise abusive adults. You are their direction, their leadership, their hope, their dreams. Always inspire them and lift them up with confidence so that they can achieve anything. My son Brandon taught me to be patient and understanding of others and to talk to people as equals. My daughter gave me wisdom that life should be looked at with love and compassion towards all. You can get so much more accomplished with a loving conversation. Children are so innocent and Godly. A kind heart goes a long way with God. My relationship with my children is so much closer as they got older and I love spending time with them. God is family.

I stopped being that person of argument and rule. I turned to God, and it's changed my life. I now listen more than I speak another Godley rule. Teach them with example. Be a God-Good example.

11
"ROUTE 91" COUNTRY FESTIVAL. WHY, GOD?

Why does God let this happen?

It was one of the deadliest shootings in American History. They named it the "Las Vegas massacre". My friends were yearly attenders at the Route 91 Country Festival in Las Vegas, Nevada.

We all had a great time together year after year, with lots of laughter and love until life unfolded in a tragic fashion.

Friday, September 29, 2017. My wife and I were in the front right side of the stage with friends, overlooking the Mandalay Bay across the street. We only stayed a short time and then returned to the VIP section. My daughter Vanessa and her friend Brittany were somewhere in the front right of the stage. We had never worried about anything there. Everyone was so nice and pleasant.

Saturday, September 30, 2017. Vanessa and Brittany went to the front of the stage early. Sam Hunt was her favorite's country singer. My wife and I were in the VIP section, ground floor down right of the stage next to general admission. I have a video of us just having such a great time that Saturday night. It was a really beautiful night that we all enjoyed so much. This was the exact area the bullets rained on innocent people one night later. The area my daughter was in that night was exactly where so many got shot and killed. It makes me sick to my stomach to this day to think about the evil that took place before our very eyes a night later.

Sunday, October 1, 2017. He did not choose Friday or Saturday night. He chooses Sunday. The day of rest and prayer. I find his choice so evil, deliberate, and calculated. Not that any day would be good to kill innocent people.

We were all excited to see Jason Aldean. We got there at 12.30 pm to wait in line. We wanted to make sure we got good seats. It was a beautiful Sunday morning. I remember thinking how nice it was. Not a cloud in the sky. You can hear sound check and vendors getting ready. We entered and walked over to get our seats. We were like a bunch of kids, trying to get to the front of the line for ice cream.

We were all so close to the stage that day. We sat under the tent and enjoyed the day, laughing and taking videos and pictures, listening to country music and loving it. We did this year after year.

Later in the afternoon, Vanessa and Brittany got tired. So we told them to come to the VIP area. They were not supposed to be in VIP that night; they only had general admission tickets. But we got the girls in. I thank God we did. Our friend that came with us for some reason kept saying to bring them into VIP over and over she kept repeating it. It was fate. My whole family was together. Otherwise, they would have been upfront near the stage where the tragedy happened. I could not imagine them not being with us when this happened. It haunts me to think of all the innocent people lost that night. God give us all free will. With that, you have choices made by evil people to kill and do wicked things.

I was prudent with my family and when I heard the first five to six shots, I moved them all behind the couches. Then the barrage

"ROUTE 91" COUNTRY FESTIVAL. WHY, GOD?

of gun fire screamed across the field. We could see bodies falling and I pushed my girls out north towards the Tropicana, away from the barrage of bullets. You could hear the bullets bouncing off the pavement. Heavy volley followed. The speakers and mics were still on at the time of the shooting, so the sound of rapid gunfire echoed all over. It sounded like the bullets were all around us. We had no idea who was shooting at us, and where they were coming from. We just headed away from the sound of the gun shots. I could see more bodies dropping as we exited the VIP tent.

My wife told the girls to pray and run, pray and run, over and over. I know that God was with us that night. As we were exiting, a guy next to my daughter got hit in the shoulder. It all happened so fast and, at that moment, I was truly frightened for my whole family. You can hear volley of bullets everywhere as it was hitting metal structures and bouncing off the pavements. The first thing I said was, God, please protect us all. God was the first thing I thought of. I pray daily after the tragedy. I pray for his merciful grace. I pray for all the families of this tragedy. We will never forget that night as long as we live. When it was all over 58 Angels had lost their lives. One more died in 2019 making the total loss 59.

I asked God, *why?* We all ask, *why, God?* Through the prophet Isaiah, God tells us, "My thoughts are not your thoughts, nor are your ways my ways" saith the LORD (Isaiah 55:8) KJV. God thinks and acts on a level different from ours. He sees things from a much broader overview.

God give us all free will.

From my perspective, it's as though we were putting together the puzzle of God with many of the pieces missing. What part of the picture are we failing to see?

Understanding why God allows evil and its resultant suffering requires a fundamental understanding of one of God's greatest gifts as well as how man has continually abused that gift. The gift is free will–or, as it is more popularly called, freedom of choice. Often the specific cause of suffering simply cannot be precisely explained–at least not in this lifetime. Sometimes, the best we can do is to accept it as explainable only by what the Bible calls "time and chance." Knowing that we live in a world awash in misery, in which tragedy can strike at any time; shouldn't we heed Christ's warning to repent and begin aligning our life with His?

There is clear evidence of this world without God…the evil that exists in souls that seek their way and their will on others. This is not God's will. He gives all free will. However, that free will can be destructive. We have all witnessed the evil will in this world. Their will to be a God has made this world evil and precarious. We all will be humbled in the end, and only He knows when that will be. Humans without God will be the demise of this world. God will have his will above all.

To my dear friends who witnessed this horrifying evil unfold in front us: Scott Pulliam, Tami Rupert, Lance Todd, Julie Todd, Tiffany Todd, Dom Cerulle, Gina Cerulle, Sierra Cerulle, Kristine Brosius, Don Kapp, and Stephanie Hauptman Kapp. This has forever changed our lives and we will never forget. We know Love always wins and we are Vegas Strong.

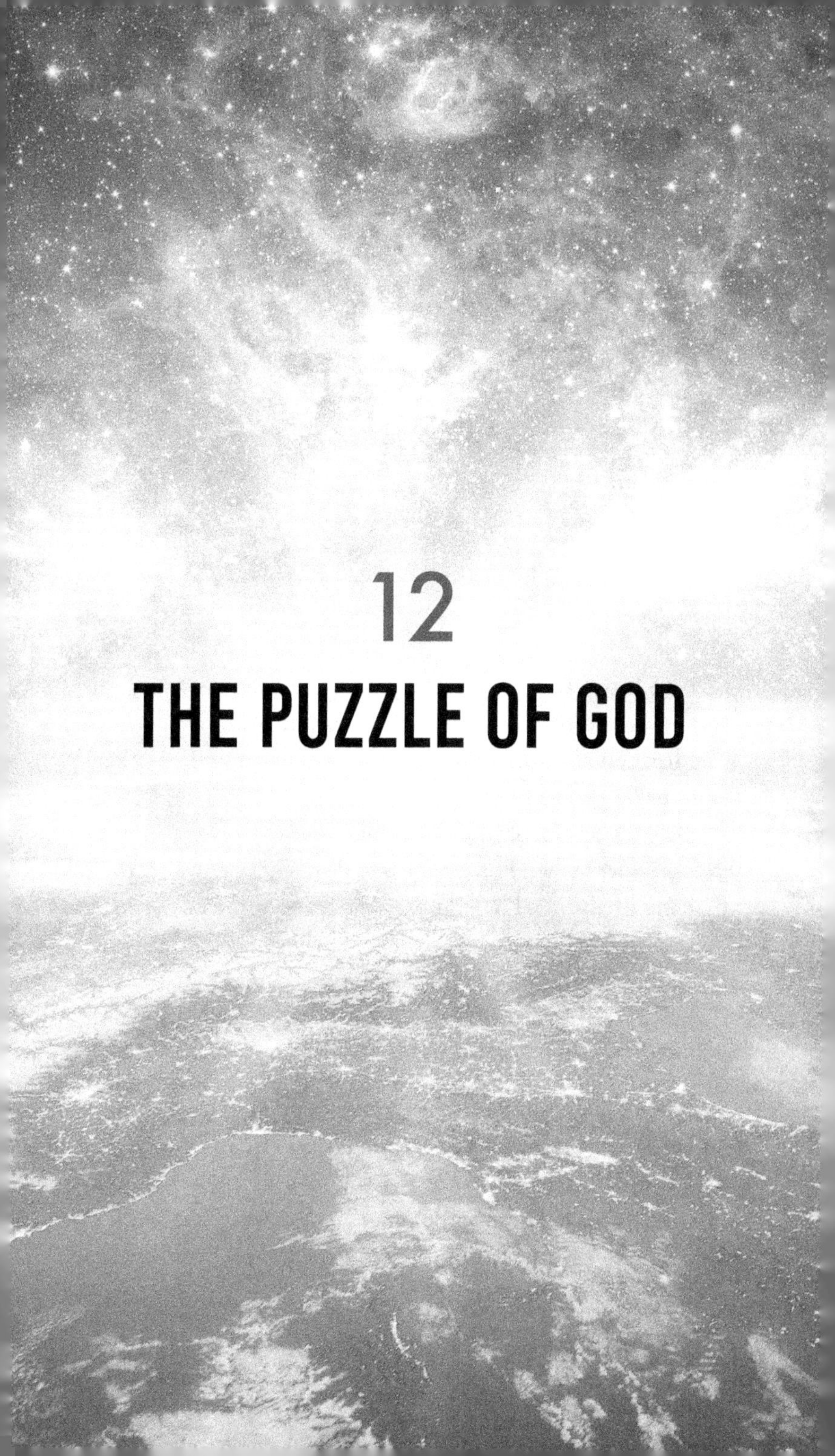

12
THE PUZZLE OF GOD

CAN YOU PUT IT TOGETHER?

God is not the puzzle. The puzzle is us not following His laws and teaching through Jesus Christ. This is what I have learned about my puzzle with God and my life. What's your puzzle with God?

Below are some sayings I love, and quotes from my mother. I refer to them when I have a cross to deal with. I consider these my little life bible. These are references to some of the most important laws God has. Maybe it will help you become a better Christian and person.

Possessions

Do not lay up for yourselves treasures on earth, where moth and rust destroy and where thieves break in and steal, but lay up for yourselves treasures in heaven, where neither moth nor rust destroys and where thieves do not break in and steal. For where your treasure is, there your heart will be also. **(Matthew 6:19–21)(KJV)**

God is Love

Giving is receiving, and to live is to love.

Unconditional love is caring about someone without limitations. It's loving without conditions and doing something to make someone happy without any thought for what we might get for ourselves.

This type of love is rare; it's uncommon to receive kindness without strings attached. This kind of love includes risk and a willingness to fail, as we give ourselves over with vulnerability.

It's putting our own needs and pride behind us and doing what's best for someone else, regardless of how we feel.

It requires staying close to someone–not judging or punishing them but loving without conditions. This type of love has the power to heal wounds, bring people closer together, and create relationships beyond our capacities to imagine.

Success

Psalm 1:1–3 says, "Blessed is the man who walks not in the counsel of the wicked, nor stands in the way of sinners, nor sits in the seat of scoffers; but his delight is in the law of the Lord, and on his law he meditates day and night. He is like a tree planted by streams of water that yields its fruit in its season, and its leaf does not wither. In all that he does, he prospers."

If you are not walking with the counsel or advice of the wicked, nor standing in the way of neither sinners nor the way that sinners are going, and are also not sitting in the seat of scoffers, then God will bless you. To be blessed means to literally "make happy." Your delight will naturally be in God's law, and you will meditate day or night. This means that like a tree planted by a stream of water, you will never wither or die but will always produce godly fruit, and everything you do will prosper. (KJV)

Addictions

Sex, porn, prostitution, drugs, alcohol abuse, stealing, killing, gluttony, and gambling are many sins to be aware of.

> *"Blessed is the man that endureth temptation: for when he is tried, he shall receive the crown of life, which the Lord hath promised to them that love him. Let no man say when he is tempted, I am tempted of God: for God cannot be tempted with evil, neither tempteth he any man: But every man is tempted, when he is drawn away of his own lust, and enticed. Then when lust hath conceived, it bringeth forth sin: and sin, when it is finished, bringeth forth death." (James 1:12–15) (KJV)*

Stomp out all addictions! Your heart must be pure to receive God's blessing. What do we do when no one is watching? God Integrity must be evident in your life. God sees all, and you can't hide your demons. Redeem and repent, and you will find glory. The battle within cannot be won unless you accept it and face it head-on.

Forgiveness

This is the toughest cross of all.

I am supposed to forgive other people who have wronged me? Stolen from me? Killed someone close to me? Gossiped about me? Lied to me? Bullied me?

We forgive by faith, out of obedience. Since forgiveness goes against our nature, we must forgive by faith, whether we feel like it or not. We must trust God to do the work in us that needs to be done so that our forgiveness will be complete.

Forgiveness frees us to move on in life. Forgive even when it hurts.

"For if you forgive men when they sin against you, your heavenly Father will also forgive you. But if you do not forgive men their sins, your Father will not forgive your sins." (Matthew 6:14–16)(NIV)(KJV)

We also forgive so that our prayers will not be hindered.

Worry

Sometimes you have to stop worrying, wondering, and doubting. Have faith that things will work out–maybe not how you planned, but just how they're meant to be.

Did you know that most people worry about things that have already happened to them? Worry not, said the Lord. He will provide all things. God is not worry. God is Faith!

Fear

Here's a memorable phrase for the acronym FEAR: "**F**eeling **E**ager **A**bout **R**eality." Reality can't hurt you. Your perception is your realty, Anthony Robbins once said to me. I believe that.

"Fear has no value in your life."

Godly traits or practices that successful people use to overcome fear.

> Focus on the present moment. Practice mindfulness of sin.
> Know the brain actually functions differently in a fearful state. Fear it, and do it anyway. That's called faith.
> They are willing to take chances with superior faith. Have a sense of vision and perspective.
> Reflect on all that is good in life and their blessings. Learn from their failures.
> Work daily with Godly direction and or fearless. Help others achieve their goals.
> Give back to those who have less.

They have confidence in their God-given abilities to succeed and move forward with their plans in faith.

The Bar Stool: Four Legs for a Balanced Life

Proverbs 11:1 says, "A false balance is an abomination to the Lord, but a just weight is his delight." (KJV)

Family = love
Spirit = God = giving = love
Body = exercise = eat right
Work = success

You need all four. Take balance seriously. Balance takes work; you must achieve this daily.

Wisdom

Wisdom, or sapience, is the ability to think and act using knowledge, experience, understanding, common sense, and insight. It's the action with the highest degree of adequacy under any given circumstance, with the limitation of error in any given action. This implies a possession of knowledge, or the seeking of knowledge to apply to the given circumstance. This involves an understanding of people, objects, events, situations, and the willingness and ability to apply perception, judgement, and action in keeping with the understanding of what is the optimal.

"The way of a fool is right in his own eyes, but a wise man listens to advice. We need to listen more and speak less. Don't be a fool that knows it all." (Proverbs 12:15)(KJV)

"God" Backward Is "Dog"

Don't you wish you could love like a dog? Animals in your life will come up to you and love you unconditionally. They don't care how your day went, how you are dressed, about your attitude, or about your demeanor. They will always give you unconditional love.

Pure love without conditions is Christ-like love. That is the meaning for God. To love God and to love people.

THE PUZZLE OF GOD

Who Is God? **G**ood, **O**bedient, **D**ivine

God is always here with you. You were created in His image, and the human body is the reflection of His work. The world was created by design. Motion was created by God. Without the motion of God, we would not exist. That motion lives in all of us.

That motion created the universe and the world we live in. That motion created all things. Jesus Christ is the clearest, most specific picture of God revealing Himself to us.

FAITH
Forward **A**ll **I**ssues **T**o **H**im.

God is present in all things in this world. Present in people, water, motion, animals, plants, and the sun. This world without evil is so beautiful by design; it's in perfect harmony. God gave us all free will to choose Him or not. The will of man to be a God in itself has made this world evil and precarious. We all will be humbled in the end and only He knows when that will be. Humans will be the demise of this world without God. God will have his will above all.

A good summary definition of God is "the Supreme Being, the Creator and Ruler of all that is, the self-existent one who is perfect in power, goodness, and wisdom." Thinking correctly about God is of utmost importance, because a false idea about God is idolatry.

I am the Alpha and Omega, the beginning and the ending, saith the Lord, which is, and which was, and which is to come, the Almighty. (Revelation 1:8)(KJV)

Live the Ten until the End

The Ten Commandments in the KJV bible are:

1. Thou shalt have no other gods before me.
2. Thou shalt not make unto thee any graven image, or any likeness of any thing that is in heaven above, or that is in the earth beneath, or that is in the water under the earth. Thou shalt not bow down thyself to them, nor serve them: for I the LORD thy God am a jealous God, visiting the iniquity of the fathers upon the children unto the third and fourth generation of them that hate me; and showing mercy unto thousands of them that love me, and keep my commandments.
3. Thou shalt not take the name of the LORD thy God in vain; for the LORD will not hold him guiltless that taketh his name in vain.
4. Remember the Sabbath day, to keep it holy. Six days shalt thou labor, and do all thy work: But the seventh day is the sabbath of the LORD thy God: in it thou shalt not do any work, thou, nor thy son, nor thy daughter, thy manservant, nor thy maidservant, nor thy cattle, nor thy stranger that is within thy gates: For in six days the LORD made heaven and earth, the sea, and all that in them is, and rested the seventh day: wherefore the LORD blessed the sabbath day, and hallowed it.

5. Honor thy father and thy mother: that thy days may be long upon the land which the LORD thy God giveth thee.
6. Thou shalt not kill.
7. Thou shalt not commit adultery.
8. Thou shalt not steal.
9. Thou shalt not bear false witness against thy neighbor.
10. Thou shalt not covet thy neighbor's house, thou shalt not covet thy neighbor's wife, nor his manservant, nor his maidservant, nor his ox, nor his ass, nor any thing that is thy neighbor's.

Look at the cross. On one side is

the word and the other is the world! Under the word are seven gifts of the Holy Spirit.

On the world side are seven capitol sins!

Take L away From World Meaning. If

You put the world first Before the word

L stands for LIE. If you Put word first L stands for Love!

Reverse the Curse, put God First!

–Rachel Klein

The most destructive habit	Worry
The greatest joy	Giving
The greatest loss	Self-respect
The most satisfying work	Helping others
The ugliest personality trait	Selfishness
The most endangered species	Dedicated leaders
Our greatest natural resource	Our youth
The greatest problem to overcome	Fear
The most effective sleeping pill	Peace of mind
The most crippling failure disease	Excuses
The most powerful force in life	Love
The most dangerous pariah	A gossiper
The world's most incredible computer	The brain
The worst thing to be without	Hope
The deadliest weapon	The tongue
The two most power-filled words	"I Can"
The greatest asset	Faith
The most worthless emotion	Self-pity
The most beautiful attire	A smile!
The most prized possession	Integrity
The most powerful channel of communication	Prayer
The most contagious spirit	Enthusiasm

–Rachel Klein

ACKNOWLEDGEMENTS

I had so many more crosses, but these have been the most important lessons for me. You will find the glory in the message of your cross, whatever that cross may be. Until you believe and trust in God with all your heart, the lesson will repeat itself over and over again until you learn it. I have learned about pride, love, money, and evil in my life. I choose God first, not last. I have learned so many lessons with my crosses. I have learned I need to seek love first, before anything else. You need to live life with *godly integrity*. What would you do if you knew God was watching?

In the simplest terms, love is God. I have learned one important thing: learn to love yourself first. That is where you will be able to create a better life for those around you. You must love *you* first. You cannot love or hate something about another person unless it reflects something you love or hate in yourself.

God gives everyone free will to choose a path in life, for better or worse. You have the choice to go with God or against God.

I believe God cares about the little things in our lives–so I pray accordingly and often end up finding God in small miracles.

Man looks at the outward appearance, but God looks at the inside–the heart of the matter. We should change our perceptions so we acknowledge miracles. It's a common problem in the media.

Some news organizations distance themselves from any reference to God, Jesus, or miracles, even when it's germane to the story.

ACKNOWLEDGEMENTS

I would like to thank my mother, Rachel and my dad Deward, who helped me become closer to God and serve God. My mother had these wonderful sayings for everything, which inspired me to write this book and use her wisdom, and I called them, "God's poetry." Because of her constant words of wisdom and advice, and God's direction, I became a better version of myself. My dad taught me to help others in need and the principals of hard work. My dad is a strong leader and great example on work ethic. My father has great integrity to do what's right always and has passed that on to me. Both parents gave me important life principals and a strong foundation for success. I am truly blessed to have them in my life. All my experiences made me who I am and I have no regrets.

Have faith in your belief in God, and your cross will be lifted. If you are not a believer, find a good Bible-based church, and go one Sunday. You may be surprised by the grace He has in store for you.

Commit to God, and He will bring you happiness you have never felt before and make your path straight. What's your cross or crosses? Write them down and stomp them out of your life one by one using lessons from the Bible. Google God with the issue you have and you will see His presence and answers to the "crosses" in your life.

I want to thank Sandra, my wife, my life, and my absolute love. She is my angel. She is a true example of God's love.

To my beautiful children, Vanessa and Brandon, you have taught me patience and love. I love you both very much. Lastly, God's creatures–our dogs, Brody, Bella, Bentley, and Martini (who passed recently), and our bird, Georgi–for the unconditional love you give us.

Thank you.

We help, we serve, we love.

God Bless,
Alan Comeaux

ABOUT THE AUTHOR

Alan Comeaux is a born-again Christian living in Ventura County, CA. He was blessed with his loving wife, Sandra, and two beautiful children, Vanessa and Brandon. He has dedicated over twenty-five years of his life to helping U.S. military veterans and homeless shelters.

www.ingramcontent.com/pod-product-compliance
Lightning Source LLC
Chambersburg PA
CBHW071024080526
44587CB00015B/2483